Sad Thoughts About A Girl

CHANTEL CHARIS

Copyright © 2017 Chantel Charis

All rights reserved.

ISBN: 1979900981
ISBN-13: 978-1979900980

PREFACE

This is a collection of poems, letters, ramblings, songs and other various writings all written to or about a specific individual from my past. They have been placed in chronological order so that one might follow the progression of these feelings, the ups and downs, and how the many different passionate emotions such as love, hatred, sadness, excitement, and so forth. I am publishing these works, despite their unrefined state, in hopes that others may find comfort in reading them.

These words are mostly written from a place of pain resulting from unrequited love, which I think is something that everyone who has ever loved can relate to. There is an added layer of discomfort and pain in these particular writings because of my stifling conflict with myself about accepting my sexuality, which was especially difficult because of the heavy influence of my family's religious background. I know that those pains are also very real and can be related to by many, and I hope that by sharing my ugly, unpleasant, and unrefined thoughts and words that those seeking empathy for similar experiences will find it here in this raw and unashamed platform, *Sad Thoughts About A Girl.*

SAD THOUGHTS ABOUT A GIRL

CONTENTS

Preface	ii
Rainbow chute 1.29.13	1
Worth Fighting For 2.17.13	5
9.3.13	6
Tunnel Out 10.23.13	9
10.31.13	12
Paws 11.1.13	19
Fonder Eyes 11.14.13	22
The Ember and the Angel 1.6.14	24
Saudade 1.17.14	26
Cave In 10.10.14	28
9.5.15	31
9.10.15	32
12.14.15	33
12.19.15	34
We Sit	37
Another Goodbye	42

CHANTEL CHARIS

Remembrance	44
1.4.16	47
1.9.16	49
1.19.16	50
1.20.16	51
1.22.16	52
Another 1.22.16	53
3.1.16	54
3.8.16	58
3.19.16	60
Amnesia (Unfinished)	63
Not My Perspective 3.24.16	67
3.30.16	69
5.17.16	71
5.18.16	73
6.3.16	75
A Golf Course, A Hill, An Over 6.16.16	77
Untitled	81
7.5.16	83

RAINBOW CHUTE
1.29.13
(A LULLABY)

Foreword: You, my dear, I give permission to dream.

Fingers sliding down the strings

Trashing out something deep

Noises screaming; indistinct

Chaos climbing; will it reach?

Finally, a broken string

Pulled from the heart so it cannot sing

Like venom and its sting

Your eyes pour and ears ring

A drop of a pin

Dink

It clatters to the ground slowly

Then rests

Silence.

You fall to the ground without a sound and tumble into what you see

The ocean swallows you whole, then you travel up the deep

Try to breathe the air but cannot; the water brings you life

You sink into a muddy place where you receive no light

An octopus wraps his arms about you in a loving way
And in the dark, his tentacles mark from where he drew
the venom

The longer held you, the less you breathed
The tighter he got, the harder it was to see
In the final moment of the dark creature
The sea retains a new feature

Black ink bleeds into the waters and the demon deceased
Dead from the disease he sucked from your head
You lose your mind and float to the top
When you regain you know where you're not

In the clouds your body lies
Covered with water drops from heaven's eyes
Misty, foggy, even hazed
Yet your vision is cut crystal clear to beyond days

You see what you must do
Don't want to follow through
You start to break the heaven's gates
Now you're falling — it's too late

You loved that sky
With wings and rays
Never wanted to say goodbye
Wanted to see beyond days

When suddenly you realize you feel the gravity
You want to fill the hole in the earth's cavity
Now, like a falling angel
You look from a different angle

If only you had a parachute
To stop the hate and the dispute
Looking at your pinky, you see a string attached
You know you have to pay a price —
Hard price to match

Falling faster than a star
You know who you are
Never wanted to face it
Now you have to taste it

You pull the last string
A pack on you explodes
Your glowing corpse comes floating down under a
rainbow
And plugs like a cork

The beauty from your rainbow chute blinds the atmosphere

Now everyone knows that the angel is here

Steadily, you lift your head and see the rain outside

You want to sob when you realize it was all in your mind

But then you see a rainbow

A sign of a promise

At that moment you know

God loves you, honest

So sleep my babe

While you can

The sun shut down his golden fan

So you can behold the face of God as you stare at the moon

And then you realize... he's staring back at you

I love you, angel

Sleep tight

And dream

WORTH FIGHTING FOR
2.17.13

The army
The navy
The marines
The air force

The plane
The tough
The boat
The horse

I held my breath
And I held back the tears
As I looked back at all the years

My fears are now tested
When I pray for you at war
And I ask myself what you're fighting for

9.3.13

Water drops roll down webbing
A ray of dusty sunlight captures colors unseen
Echoes them around the whole room
Like a prism being set on fire
It explodes and splinters your heart with color

That's how it begins for you
It aches and rejects the beauty
The beauty turns black and it hardens the muscle
That housed these mysterious glassy sheets

The muscle quit exercising and beauty began to fight
The heart began to quit feeling and became weak
So weak it began to cry tears of black blood
Blood is only black if it's been waiting too long

And these tears were long past due to be shed
And shed they were till there were no more

The heart didn't make anymore bloody tears
And the corpse which housed this muscle became cold
Cold with fear and confusion and unanswered questions

Confused by how the glassy prism could have exploded on you
You begin to ask questions which you alone can begin to answer

The fear of the answers you'll find keeps you silent

But it becomes more than fear — it becomes torture
You sit alone in the dark empty room with the webs
You begin to realize, but not face, that this is the pain of the caterpillar's transformation

You were caught up in your webs and when the light and liquid exploded, it set you free
Even though it feels quite the opposite

You're trapped in your raccoon and can't get out
You were once comfortable there, without the light
Without the air — the world around you

But now, you're wishing you would have been destroyed by the spider which held onto what it could of you
Your wrapping and silky woven sleeve
Saved your life, though you know it not

For when you were trapped among the webs,

A firm loving hand plucked you from there and tightly rolled you into a test

A test you still don't know about, and maybe never will

Now you struggle and attempt to break free of your trapping test

You're just not finished yet— you're almost ready

You're so close you can taste the air and it makes you sick that you can't breathe it

That's why you're going to be such a beautiful butterfly

THE BEGINNING.

TUNNEL OUT
10.23.13

Is this the tunnel out?
Nothing will ever be forgotten about

Give yourself one more day
Before you take your life away

There's this glow that I see
Or rather, it sees me

I feel it in my bones
A feeling no one knows

Because everyone feels differently
Wish I felt this fervently

I've been digging for years
While burying my fears

And now that I must face it all
I don't slip — I feel a fall

Never will this battle stop
Not even when my guard drops

Always try to get the best of me
Never let the sadness flee

I'm going to try to get the best of it
It will try to kill when it sees fit

But the light I'm imagining
Is actually happening

And do I see the exit sign?
Am I dreaming it's mine?

Scratching with my nails
Scraping through muddy veils

Then there's this hope
I won't exit, but I will cope

Still very confused and skeptical
But warming under your spectacles

You see that under a fine glass
No happiness can ever last

But that's okay with me I think
Sadness allows happiness to sink

Making it sweeter than ever when it returns
And the lowness of humanity sometimes burns

There is a tunnel out I've heard
Where sun shines and you hear the birds

Today is not the beginning or end
Just when I realize adventure's my friend

Because that's what I've longed for
It's made my mind sore

But I've been caught up in adventure
Since the day of departure

From above the earth and feeling high
Feeling like I was above your sight

So now that I'm far below it
I see the tunnel out of it

No time to waste or think past
Hurry up before you're last

Don't sit around in waiting
Can't walk around in hating

10.31.13

Your body is a paint brush
Your shadows dance and blush
Feet don't even pad gently
You're floating through the dust

It's not all in your head
It's better left unsaid
Chills run down your spine
This feeling left unread

Body twists and slashes
Mind cleared and love crashes
Not even you exist
Its beauty harasses

So untouchable and only real
You can enter but you can't feel
Let the rain come pouring down
The momentary dream seals

No happy or sad face
No limits of time or space
Let yourself become entranced
Can't remember or erase

Spell your name with your toes
Twirl and think what no one knows
Close your eyes for just a second
Where did your exhale go

Pursed lips, rolling hips
Pointed feet, light tips
Heavy sighing and tears
Spinning head and deep dips

Twisted heart wrenches
Soul craves and quenches
No way to explain
Blood stains and stenches

Scarred toes and ankles
Heavy weight yet angels
You're flying down on earth
A dream only to make real

Nothing heard or seen
Silence wraps you in your scene
No count or score or page
It's your mind poured out, queen

No crown to top or dress to cover
The beauty is what's under
Love made in silence
How else would you be discovered

Hair wisps and brushing
Body painting and touching
Music heard through the silence
Finished and then nothing

A stare dead in the eye
A tear but not a cry
Feet hanging up the dream
Fall to the ground — die

Dipped in paint you dance
Before you die you get one chance
Let it all out and live your moment
Don't waste time to prance

Passionately speak through
No words, but the way you move
Listen to no air as you go
Was it different as you flew?

Please don't wait another day
This moment won't stay
Sing, my angel, sing
There's no other way

Feel from within, pulling out
Reach inside; grab with no doubt
Pluck the heart's hair strings
Don't plug the leaking spout

Let your thought and beauty drip
No one's worthy to drink or sip
You're lovely, don't believe otherwise
You slash yourself with your whip

Oh angel, your scars are much better
The rain doesn't make you wetter
You're already drenched in fears
But beauty is a haze around your fetter

Ball and chain around your neck
Slips into a sloping wreck
But it's crooked like a crane
Crash the surface with attack

But glide and swish and dive
Let me know you're still alive
Give yourself the room to swim
One, two, three, four, five —

Sit till dawn in the mist
None knew of you so none missed
None but me, myself, and I
My soul you kissed

Never can you ever die
Never would I ever tell you a lie
Never can you fade
Hold a stare, start to cry

Your eyes are deep and dream
Gateway to your soul's seem
Rip it open, share what's inside
I know it's black, but it beams

I know that there's more to you
Never will you see you through
But I will never let you go
I looked one moment and you grew

I can't give up just yet
You've said things I can't forget
It's changed my world
You've built me and gotten me set

"Now fly straight," you say
"Fly back another day,"
You call along, but you're ahead
Your brain just doesn't sway

It's always on a track
Never ever looking back
Singing and sobbing
It races; never slacks

Cut loose your strings
Stand back; let yourself sing
Fingers weave and tangle
Soon you've grown your wings

No need to die now, you're complete

No need to even dance with feet

You're flying on earth

A dream only to compete

PAWS
11.1.13

Please don't leave me even after I look better
I will never be strong enough to stand on my own
I have a drawer full of masks waiting to be burned
But I'll take this one off just to let you know
That I'm not steadily beating anything but thought
And this smile is a face just for those that don't care
And I might look just dandy, but trust me, I'm not
People are judgmental and it's just not fair
Smoke making me cry, it's just a lie
The tears are glowing on my roses
Eyelids so thin you see my white eyes
Wrap up in wool to look just nice and cozy
Keep me breathing through the sub-zero dark
Tell me to stay awake so that I don't fade away
Wrap your paws around my beating heart
You know when you leave I'll tell you to stay
Don't let me down now; you're all I've got
I know that we're all hanging by a thread
It's unravelling; don't tell me it's not
The music is scrambling in my head
And the needle is crackling on the vinyl
Tangled up in my sheets in my sinking bed
It's something unfinished, but it's final

So wrap your paws around these fibers
Hide my face in your furry neck and shoulder
Glowing tears fall; darkness is a bad hider
It soon becomes warmer in the dark
Because a glow in the darkness is all that I have
Keep feeding the glow with little sparks
Rub my thin hazed eyes with balm and salve
Wipe my tears till your coat heats and glows
My word, I'm cold; I won't last for sure
You slip your grip and the warmness goes
Your paws are realities and comforts, not cures
Soft and leathery pads of black and grey
I'm shivering now with fear and cold death
Grab my sweater and help me start to sway
Whisper in my ear and let me feel your breath
Or just let me hear your breathing
No words need be said or dreamt
It's keeping me alive and believing
Just touch and warm me up; I'm drenched
I may be glowing but the lies are showing
You can tell I'm not okay and need your paws
Squeeze this twig between your arms
Breathe out as you break the pause
I know I'm not safe from any harms
But you are there which makes hurt hide
Because you can see beneath the hurt

You see what's invisible; what's inside
Not like the others when I have to burry my cuts
You try to stitch them up and patch up my heart
Search frantically on your calloused paws
To find every shattered and scarred part
Now I'm no longer afraid of world's harm
I know that you love me and it's beautiful
I feel pain flow out and into your embracing arms
You breath into my sails and now they're full
Aim me skyward and point towards the horizon
Throw me into a testing wind and blazing fire
Plant a seed in my heart and imagine a scion
See me sink but scream after me "higher"
I know if I fall, your paws will catch me
I know if I dream, you will imagine and believe
Along my side I wish you'd stand and see
That I'm not healed, I'm just relieved

FONDER EYES
11.14.13

You look at her with eyes of curiosity
Not thinking that she looks at you with depth
Every time you turn your shoulder
She stares at the ground beneath

You hear the words that she speaks
Not listening to anything she means
Every time you give a glance or a smile
She begin to feel helpless and weak

You hear of the things that she means
Not by her but by other tones of voice
Every time you hear of that girl
She sounds in love without choice

You glance with the mention of her name
Not noticing her most of the time
Every time she sees your eyes
She knows the walls she'll have to climb

Confused and feeling hostile you stare
But she returns your look with fonder eyes
Suddenly it all is in your front of you there
And you walk away full of surprise

She turns away and walks out for good
You turn around and look on to her
If you had the strength you would
Stare at her with fonder eyes

THE EMBER AND THE ANGEL
1.6.14

11.11.13: Once there was an angel that befriended a dimming ember. And they lived instead of dying. (Though this ember glows faint, it glows all the same.)

Though she was an angel, she still knew her demons. And they knew where she stayed. She was sent on a mission to their heaven; her hell. They loved her and didn't want to let her go. In this hell, she observed the fire, the lava, the coals, the embers and ash, the smoke and the flame. But among all this, she found an ember that was not like the others. It was more faint than any of the others. She looked over her shoulders to make sure no one was watching, then she picked it up, blew it off, and looked into it. With her breath it grew warmer and possessed a burst of light, but nothing very bright. Again it faded and the angel stuffed it in her pocket. Sometimes this ember burned her, but she still kept it in her pocket and times asked God to give her a puff of life to make her ember glow. The angel was warned by this glowing object that someday the faint vibrancy and warmth would leave, and she would become like a cold rock, only weighing her down. The angel did not want to believe her though. So the angel's mission lasted a longer time than it was meant to. Her father, God, called her back to heaven, but she could not go yet. She was not allowed to go back to heaven with the of hell she kept in her pocket always. This angel did not want to give up her ember. But she had two choices. One: she could give up her ember; leave it to whatever its fate may be, and go back to paradise. Two: stay in her hell with a virtually lifeless rock weighing her down to the bone. If she chose the relief. The choice is hers. This ember just needed her to know how much she's sorry and how much she's weighing her down; keeping her from soaring. She's sorry, I promise. But maybe her fate was to grow cold so that the angel could go back to heaven, her home, and ember would have no more pain and wouldn't have to endure another moment of hell. Ember is keeping Angel from completing her mission.

Sincerely,

~~A Demon~~ Observer on Fire

SAUDADE
1.17.14

Where are you?

My mind has been engraving your name into my heart.

Who are you?

My spirit told me that you were it's missing part.

You are lost.

You can't find your way home anymore.

You are a void.

You're like the air in a room without a floor.

When did you...?

A long time ago. You weren't there for me then.

Why did you...?

For reasons you will never know. It was before, friend.

I want you.

But I know I can't have you ever in this life.

I love you.

But I can't say that when I'm holding this knife.

Do you pray?

Yes, but only when I believe in listeners.

Do you listen?

Yes.

I found you.

But that was before you slipped away again.

I lost you.

So I've given up and have become saudade.

TO: MY ANGEL
CAVE IN
10.10.14

I thought I was lonely before. Lies. The floor feels more company than I. Given, it's walked all over being used only as a foundation for everything else, but I hate being by myself. I thought I was an introvert, but I only have introvert tendencies forced upon me from infancy. Always being told that I can and cannot do and never allowed to love who I gravitate towards. Now I gravitate toward the floor. So I lay upon it with my ear against the ground in hopes of hearing its heart pound. I need a sign of life. Because I am no longer living. Merely existing in the static of air. Writing love songs to someone who isn't there. Running to someone who has never been. Hoping the only thing I love doesn't cave in. The confusion that plagued me years ago lay dormant for a cycle of time, but we all know that dormant doesn't mean dead. I don't kill it. They always told me to be gentle. Don't kill it they'd say. But then it'll come back some day. And since I don't hate it, it's not dead. And it's back. It never knocks, it knows the door is open. Confusion brings in his panic attacks and unpacks the fear and doubt, stuffing it in the cubbies of the hide out in my mind. So while you're staring out the window, thinking of ways to behave, I'm thinking of ways to escape. I don't want to fix it. You do. Somehow, I know you'll get through this. We've gone unnoticed without a hitch for years on end, but now is the time you must promise me, you won't cave in. You weren't caught; you raised the white flag. Of course there are stipulations, but they must be complied to when your life is at stake. I got found out by a hound who doesn't know where their snout belongs. They can't keep it out of the crotches of little girls and boys who pet the beast to make them happy. They didn't clean up well enough. They are messy, messy children. They have too much trust for that silent mutt with the glazed eyes. Someday they will learn to despise the hound. But it'll be the result of regret. Congratulations darling, you didn't forget strategy and practicality. I was living in a reality that no one else could see. We're both confined to deal with our demons, but you have a construction team working on you. Building you up and chipping away the waste. Tearing down the walls you thought couldn't be moved. Maybe they're being replaced, but they are being worked on. I have to listen to the shrieks of unsatisfied customers that come to me seeking answers that I don't have. I don't know what's happening inside this mad mind. I only know what I miss. I'm not sure where to go from here. I didn't ask for this. The confusion dwelling within me conceived a child and named her fear. She loves to dance around in my eyes and every time I look at you, she spins on her toes. What she doesn't realize is that I'd be willing to bend over backwards just to look at you differently. I'm not as limber as I used to be. But I'm more willing than ever. Sometimes I like to forget her because she doesn't let me enjoy you the way you deserve to be enjoyed.

9.5.15

I remember your face like it was the moon
Like every day compared to yours was merely a star
forming constellations around your being

I would like to think that I was the sun, sharing my light
for you to reflect

Only, I know it isn't true

9.10.15

You say "I'm drifting" as if sleep is an endless ocean and you are but a piece of pollution floating into the horizon of unconsciousness.

12.14.15

It's that moment
When you realize that you're over it
That no matter how much back peddling you do
It won't fix anything
At all

It won't fix anything at all

Because it's a moment
Just like when you realize you're falling for it
No matter how many sleepless nights you fight
It doesn't make the other party involved fall too
It won't fix anything
At all

12.19.15

I coughed up my left lung for you
And that side of my chest collapsed
Because you already stole my heart

I didn't actually cough up my lung for you
But you drown me in your artificial affection
And left me swimming inside myself

I now face a certain death:
A lie
Or asphyxiation

The reason I decided to add my lung to your arsenal
Is because I know what it's like
To have a heart skip a beat
And suffocation rise like flames fed by gasoline

I know you can't help it

So take this sopping sponge
Set it beside that throbbing chamber

But beware —
The sponge will soon dissolve
And the chamber is already broken
So take what you want from me
While you still can

remembrance

I remember
The whispers in my ear
You said "I love you" over and over and over again
Now I wish I couldn't hear

I can feel this
Your fingers through my hair
So I cut it all off
But I still keep the locks
In a box
Under my bed…

Because I can't let you go

I remember
The Angels in the snow
You gave me your hand
As I stepped on the ice
We promised not to let go

I no longer love you
The way that I loved you
Maybe you hate me
I'm hoping
You'll say it
Again one more time
With feeling

WE SIT

We sit.
We sit alone in the dark. We sit alone in the dark silently.
We silently sit on the pavement.

The stars are shooting me.
Piercing me.
Crossing my eyes.
Star crossed lovers.
But I can never say "we were" because it was only I.

We sit.
We sit alone in the dark.
We sit alone but together in the dark.
We sit together knee deep in the snow.

The clouds are suffocating me.
Drowning me.
Pulling wool over my eyes.
Blind lovers.
But I can never say "we were" because it was only I.

We sit.

We sit in the shadows.

We sit together in the shadows.

We sit unbuckled in the backseat of my car.

The street lights are blinding me.

Killing me.

Exposing thoughts in my mind I wish they wouldn't shed light on.

Not lovers.

And I can always say "we were" because it was true.

We sit.

And as we sit I fight wars with myself. I consider the euphoric joy I experience from your silence.

From your companionship even though we are alone and silent.

I consider the beautiful utterances that fall from your soft, soft lips when you speak in these silences and I consider how they make me feel complete, and one with the earth.

One with you.

We sit.

And as we sit, I reach into my soul's abyss, searching for the right words.

And the right words are very hard.

I pull out these words and they crumble from my tongue as if I'm parched and weak.

"I love you. I would die for you."

And the silence that follows affirms the "we" was only ever I. I am we. I am the never. I am the silence.

I am alone.

We sit.

So as I sit alone,

I cannot forget that you are my pearl and I am your clam.

You are the beautiful treasured part of me that I desperately wanted to be "we."

So I reach inside myself.

I reach into my soul's abyss,

Searching for the umbilical chord.

And as I find it, I know this won't be easy. I pull you out, my pearl.

The chord is wrapped around your neck.

And look, it's now wrapped around mine.

I snip the chord and tie the lifeline on your side.

And we sit.

Only I am dying, my sweet pearl.

But worry not,

For you were my world.

I know, my pearl, that you meant no harm. But what good am I, without a world to die in?

So I will sit here alone, alive.

Because to die for you would be to prove my love. And I am weak and discouraged already.

I cannot end this misery.

My pearl,

Just please only know that you loved me more and

You were right.

I am a coward and will stay here.

I will sit,

Alone, alive.

I'm sorry my pearl,

Forgive me, your clam.

Sometimes I don't know how to open;

Most times, I don't know who I am.

But you kept me wishing,

Wanting,

Waiting,

Hoping for the sitting to last forever.
I know I am alone, alive.
I want you to do better.
Goodnight, my pearl.
I love you.
I would live for you.

And here we sit.
Alone but together.

I sit.

You sit.

We sit.

ANOTHER GOODBYE

Blinking, glowing windows, popping up into my vulnerability. Small dings in my ears and blue bubbles illuminating in the corner. Why did you speak to me? You say you still don't know.

Presence, yet ignorance. He owned you. You let him. You loved it. Splits in the snow, hat strings in your hands, cheeky grins. Your eyes felt like glass marbles rolling into me, your pile of jacks. Why didn't you speak to me? I won't ever ask you.

Pills and blueberries, tears and PTSD, sick jokes and PG13 movies when the only thing we'd been allowed to see was Finding Nemo. I shared every grimy detail of my existence with you. We laid in the road and made angels in the snow. Why didn't you ever tell me anything? You won't answer that question.

We are together, yet forbidden to speak. You're sitting across the table, but just out of reach. I learn to read your eyes, those warm yet glassy globes. You began to tell me everything, and then I realized why you never answered my previous question.

A birthday comes, a birthday goes. Another birthday comes, and goes, only this time, no one knows you left with it. Not even me. I sit alone in a theatre, staring.

Staring at blinking, glowing, windows, destroying my vulnerability. I have lost control, and so have you. You said we could be together. You said I understood. You said. But yet, you never said. Why didn't you tell me? I'll never see you again.

REMEMBRANCE

I remember

The whispers in my ear
You said "I love you," over and over and over again
Now I wish I couldn't hear

I can feel this
Your fingers through my hair
So I cut it all off
But I still keep the locks
In a box
Under my bed…

Because I cannot let you go

My heart used to skip beats
To overcome the feelings of love
But now when they skip
It's mostly because
I'm hoping
You'll say it
Again, one more time
With feeling

I remember
The Angels in the snow
You gave me your hand
As I stepped on the ice
We promised not to let go

My heart used to skip beats
To overcome the feelings of love
But now when they skip
It's mostly because
I'm hoping
You'll say it
Again, one more time
With feeling

I cannot believe
The words that I see
On a lighting up screen
When you're over there
And I'm over here
And the saddest part is
I think that I'm over you

I don't want to let go
The fear of the unknown
Is keeping me under
The tides of the future
The past, and the present
I'm dying but don't let
That keep you here

I no longer love you
The way that I loved you
Maybe you hate me
I'm hoping
You'll say it
Again, one more time
With feeling

1.4.16

Meet me by the door
Put your shoes on
Don't try to tie them
    Up   like you did
With us

Leave your sorry soul
Under the welcome mat
Don't come back
    Like you did before

I can't breathe when you're here
I can't breathe when you're gone
So I will suffocate
And fall into your arms
There are sheets of white
Over the chairs and the lights
Because all you left here
Were ghosts of you

I can't go back
To the time you told me that
Our lives were permanent
They're not

My eyes have found the window
I can't always let go
With you staring
In my eyes

Leave your rusted watch
I've cried too many times
Watching the time pass
    As if we don't have enough

1.9.16

It's not right
It doesn't hurt anymore
I'm just disappointed
Fed up with all the lies
You said you had things to do
I get it
But I see what those things are
And you're not alone
And I'm not with you
And it just kills me to think
You think I can't handle the truth
That you don't love me
Even though I love you

1.19.16

She said "when I was a girl…"
I said "what are you now?"
She said "I am a man."

1.20.16

Sometimes you know it's love
But there's nothing you can do about it

So you don't do anything about it
And you think that's the way it should have to be anyways

But then you find out it's not
And maybe you were never in love at all

And you begin to question everything you thought you knew about love

And that's how I lost you

1.22.16

You drive me like a motive drives a mass murderer

Two brown eyes stare straight into mine
They cut my head into two bloody slices

My heart doesn't notify if it's still beating
Or if it's fleeting

And all I know is that I feel like I'm living in the realm of
death
But I am more alive than I have ever been
That's the only way I know how to explain it

ANOTHER 1.22.16

They are drawn to hues of blues and reds

Metal balls with three holes roll down like heads
Spinning from the confusion and beautiful illusion
Of the hues of blues and reds on the other two heads

And here I am
Writing about them again
Even though I swore I would not

3.1.16

Let's be happy together

Let us mock the sun for the way it kills and grows and shows things over time as it moves darkness around to expose the lines between the lines.

Let's laugh at the pre-sunrise "what ifs" and cry because of the post sunset recollections.

Let's lay in the middle of the street and kiss, knowing that the stars encourage our type of affection.

Let's crawl through windows and pretend our feet aren't stained from asphalt that we "most definitely did not walk on tonight because we've been in bed."

Let's tell the truth, because we were in bed. Tangled in miles of white cotton that are the perfect transparency for us to see each other smile.

Synchronized sighing and toe wiggling keep time to our thoughts as they spin like the earth on its axis. Spinning us access to the secrets of our existence.

The axis is invisible, but we are true. You are truly beautiful and let us remain us as we were that night.

Let's split the silence with our shallow breaths that scream "I am here."

Let's run with our bare feet till they bleed and let's cast shadows of immortal images till our knees buckle and our hearts give out and then let us shout and kick at the sky and ask the world why it let us let ourselves down.

Let's be in love together…

Let us let our souls wander into the chambers of another and let them be crushed like green shells on walnuts. Let them be devoured like peony buds are by ants. Let them indulge in their craving for chance. Let us let our souls wander.

Let's be in love together even if it's not with each other.

Let's compare our butterfly collection from our intestines that we pinned to our sleeves after realizing hearts are too raw to be used as fashion accessories.

Let's stay alive together…

Let's not forget that every night was a tentative goodbye for so long that hello became our savior and you are still my angel — thank you for let me be your ember.

Let's not take for granted any longer the breath we breathe to silently scream the things we feel so deeply.

Let's be the rope we both hold onto as a safety line. I have your end and you have mine. Let's never let go; it's the tiny moments that remind me we are full of infinite momentum as long as we hold on for each other. I swear I'll never let go.

Let's hold onto the letters death left behind to remind us that she is coming one of these nights. Let's read them together every once in a while, because I never want to forget what it's like to be alive with you.

Let's be together…

Let us find the beginning of our hands as we are far too familiar with each other's finger tips from forcibly slipping away over years and weeks and days apart I still feel together with you.

Let's create our own reality where time and distance have no say in the time we distance our auras only slightly so they do not create atomic warfare.

Let's hold hands and run in the tall grass kissed by evening dew. Let's sit in a room whose walls are made of windows and make music that eyes can dance to.

Let's lay in the field and question the world and its existence so boldly that the moon not only smiles, but laughs with jealousy of our undeniable unity and life.

Let's not forget that we are so alive.

Let's die together.

Let us leave this earth to enter another dimension where the distance between us is immeasurable because it does not exist. Let's run away from tomorrow and yesterday and today. Let's run away from concept, where bliss is unobtainable and happiness is a myth. Let's run away from our parents and the troubles they missed. Let's run into each other, because I miss you and I could use a hug.

Let us be scattered to the same wind and let us never settle on any mediocre hill; let us rest on a mountain where we can see the sun and all that it does.

Where we can laugh at the way we mocked it once, even though that's what killed us. Let silent life grow in our soil so that our stories will remain untold, but those like the sun will know we were here.

3.8.16

Every time I eat vanilla ice cream, I want to sit with you in a hole filled with boiling water, peeling back our dead skin. We stare at the stars and don't speak and it's painfully heavenly. The tears that roll down my cheeks are salty and warm like the water they drop into. You really can't tell if I'm crying or not unless you're looking at the surface, and we both know you're too deep for that. I love the feeling of cold ice cream melting on my tongue and nose, the smell of vanilla wafting in the steam rising from this hole we sit in. But there's a man from the second floor in the window watching and smelling the steam as its wafting and there's not a thing we can do about it.

Every time I wear that pink dress I want to dance with you one more time. I want to feel your cheek pressed up against mine and the heavy breaths to fill the space between us. There are 28 + 8 eyes staring at you and I, but two look away and the others in dismay cannot help but stare at the way that our hands fit perfectly together and our figures are complimentary. No one can deny our smiles as we are completely aware of the that we will take, yet we dance in our bare feet on splintering wood, burning it up. This is the only three minutes of three years that we will remove our masks. Three minutes of three years that I refuse to give back. Three minutes of three years that you and I saw what it could have been like if we were together, satisfied.

3.19.16

It's mid May and we lay and we lay
The windows are open
The screens are torn
Symphonies of insects and the smell of dirt poison the air
Star upon star lean down to my soul and poke holes in my
heart
They steal and they house these holes in my heart and my
soul with light
Untarnished, pure, liquid light
It is weightless, it isn't painless, it is suffocating
And with every breath I take
I feel as if I am drowning in this light

It's mid May and we lay and we lay
In the darkness
As I am drowning in light
And it's inside but it's out
And I'm inside but I'm inside out
And the outside is coming inside go out!

It's mid May and we lay and we lay

Is that the wind, the soft evening breeze?

Or is that the whisper of death speaking to me?

I feel as though every inhale I partake of could be my last

My chest rises and falls

And every time it falls, it sinks just a little deeper into the twenty three year old mattress dressed in pink sweaty sheets

It's mid May and we lay and we lay

And I'm dying

I can feel it

My air is escaping and never returning

My past time is unravelling before my fluttering eyelids that are held together by baby blue and deep purple veins

My present time does not exist

And my future time is only a distant memory of something I once imagined could be

I smell the earth and I close my eyes

The symphony subsides and I wonder why

It's mid May and we lay and we lay

It begins to rain

The earth stops shaking

The leaves fall down with the weight of the stars crying "here we are here" and "there we are there" and "souls full of holes are no longer souls so let us fall like the hops of those that wish upon us every night one of us decides to shine bright enough to be seen" and maybe that's why people don't shine bright enough to be seen

And I only feel the cold air sit still above my mouth as if it's too sweet and pure for me to partake of one last time

So I exhale and

My body sinks into the mattress I think is comfortable and

It's mid May and we lay and we lay

And you've been asleep the whole time

Because you're doing fine and your chest doesn't rise or fall

It just is

Like the tide

And I'm dying

I'm not dead

It's mid May and we lay and we lay

And I'm alive

AMNESIA (UNFINISHED)

I loved you
I love you
I never hated you
I hate you
I love you
I want to love you
The way that I used to
Love you

But that was then
And I can no longer remember
How I loved you

What was it then?
That captivated you?
Was it all a lie?

You captivated me

What did we talk about?
What did we think about?
Where did we go?

You left
I'm not mad
It's just fact

I spent the last three
Years of my life
Erasing moments
As they took place

Everything we did
Or wanted to do
Or could have done
Could have been
Could have wanted
Could have been amazing
But I do not remember

I'm sorry that
I cannot remember

I feel like a victim of war
Come home with amnesia
A blow to the head
PTSD

People greet me with

Smiles

Tears

Gifts

Hugs

Kisses

A first

Open arms

Closed doors

Locked cupboards

Baby gates

Chain link fences

It all makes sense now

But I still cannot remember a thing

You were there

I was there

But I don't remember

And you won't tell me

So how can I be sorry

When I don't know

What I've done

Or what I haven't done

Why am I sorry
And you're not?
Why are things different?
For you
For me

Why are they different?

I don't remember

NOT MY PERSPECTIVE
3.24.16

She was always a mess

Scabs on her face

Dried blood under her fingernails

Her heart throbbed until

It crumbled

And pieces of it cluttered the floor

Like words in my mind that I wanted to say to her

But never did

Her heart used to say something

She used to be someone

But now it is broken and disorganized

Watching her fix herself

Was like watching her play scrabble

And towards the end of the game

Just when only one tile remains

She shuffles them all

Scattering letters and destroying any words that once were

I watch

She lines up the tiles

To form new words

This is my favorite part

First there was chaos

Now, a new heart

3.30.16

You make me want to smoke until my lungs turn black and
my face turns white

You make me want to run in circles while my life stands
still

You make me want to climb to the top of a building only
to see if the blood rushes to my feet as they dangle from
the edge

You make me want to write words about you that I
wouldn't dare speak aloud, yet make me feel as though
whatever I say will never be good enough

You make me feel important, yet insignificant

You make me feel insignificant

I spend a day and eight hundred nights spending air and
tears trying to remember how you made me feel the way I
feel

You make me want to destroy myself and call it art, yet at
the same time, become the best I can be in order to stand
apart

You make me want to stop time, yet rewind it even though
the past was ugly
Even though the past was ugly
Even though the past was ugly, we were together
We were together
But I cannot remember
I cannot remember
Remember?

5.17.16

Spend another Christmas with me. Wait, what about the children? Spend another day without him, the monster in your brain. Love me like you said you would. Wait, what did you think of me when we first met? Spend another new year with me. We never had that kiss. I swore that I was the one you were in love with when you were holding my hand. Wait, what about the time you told me so? Spend another day in bed with me. Wait, did you ever sleep? Neither did I. Wait, what about your father? Wait, what about my mother? Wait, what about sleep? Spend another night awake with me. There are lights in the window shining from the street and laughter coming from behind the fence and those are our children and this is our home and the shadows dancing in the street are the only monsters we have to face anymore. We can close the windows and the curtains and lie next to each other and hold onto memories being made and the awful things that have happened will be made small by the ever present fall that you and I descend together. That's what love feels like. Spend another night away and I swear. I swear to god. I cannot any longer. Wait, what about me? That's not important. Wait, what about us? Maybe you never loved me. Maybe this all was a lie. Maybe I always loved you.

Maybe you knew and didn't want to break my heart. Maybe I'm a fool for knowing you didn't love me and going along with it. Maybe I'm a fool for still caring and wishing you the best. Wait, what about you? Silence.

5.18.16

I'm trying to push you far out of my thoughts
Like the ocean heaving up pollution onto once heavily
populated beaches
People used to just sit and watch
Throw
Sit and watch
Slow
Slower
Stop
No one visits them anymore

I think and I think of all the time we spent together
And I let the memories rush in and out
But some of them never make it out
They rush down busy highways
Blow red lights
Blow my brains out
Blow red red lights behind my eyes
My brain is out
And I track them down as they dead down
Dark and crowded allies
Turning left then left
And all that's left is to force them out

So I follow them down

And force them out

Like cars being spit out one way streets

The thought of you is finally leaving me

And it can never come back

Come back

6.3.16

I have a line
You have a line

Yours is supposedly parallel to mine

But I'll stick around
In case somewhere down the line
Yours and mine
Intersect

I love swinging till the chains become parallel with the ground
I love climbing ladders until I run out of rungs
I love chasing the sunset until it melts itself away
So, in those ways, I guess you could say that I'll be around till the end
Or at least until our paths are sure not to cross

But maybe one day, I'll find myself kissing the dirt
Or climbing so high that I intersect with the sun
And can breathe the dusk and the dawn before they melt away

Until then, you will be

A line supposedly parallel to me

And the funny thing about parallel lines

Is that yours can be so utterly close to mine

But unless we are proven false

You will always be just out of reach

A GOLF COURSE, A HILL, AN OVER
6.16.16

There is a bridge

We will never cross it

We agree to that

So let's lay down

Let's fall asleep under the glowing darkness

Or not

Tell me

Okay fine

Sorry

Go ahead

Yes

You can ask again, but the answer is the same

Yes, she was the only one I loved

Yes, she was the only one I was in a relationship with

Yes, I want to be loved someday

Yes, I am okay with being loved by someone

But tell me

What does it feel like

What does it mean

What do the silences mean

Tell me

I can't imagine a world where I feel comfortable loving and
being loved by the same person

I don't know a place to find someone to accept me as I am

I don't know who I am enough to be accepted as I am

Tell me

What is it like to be so nourished that you can see straight, yet be so encompassed by a mutual passionate feeling that you can't make out faces

Tell me

What is it like to be touched by softness and care

I don't know what it's like to be in the same room as someone you love and feel comfortable enough to say it

What is it like to be in the same room as someone you love and not have to say a single word for everyone to know your love

You love so much that the plants turn away from you to look straight into the sun so as not to be burned

What is it to be loved

Tell me

I don't know what a kiss feels like on my lips

What do hands do besides grope and harm

What do four eyes look at when they're alone

I don't know what it's like to be sober and held

So yes, I've had a relationship

But it doesn't count because the feelings were forced and never double sided

So you can keep trying to crack me

To get inside my rib cage and ease the internal bleeding

But I don't know if there's anything left to crack

Because I think the internal bleeding has left me dead

But let's keeping watching the clouds turn purple and stay sitting on the moon's face

Let's count the fireflies one more time so we could say we counted the stars and cracked the heavens wide open (please don't split my ribs open — I've always been in a cage)

And keep telling me over and over again that you're a safe place

Please say it again because I can't believe you

Please say it as many times as I've heard I'm going to hell and then again and again

Please tell me you'll accept me and love me for who I am as many times as I've been told to disown myself and make me listen like I did to them

Please keep making me believe everything is going to be okay and I'll find love

Please tell me I will be loved

Please tell me over and over again until I remember those words because I've never heard them before and they're new to me and I want to remember them

Please tell me over and over and over again

Over and over and over and over and over again

This isn't about getting over her

No

Tell me

This is about something else

Let's keep looking at the clouds till they move out of the way

No, not my feelings

The clouds

The clouds

Not my feelings

The clouds

Tell me

Over and over and over and over and over again

UNTITLED

I pondered for a while before realizing

It was 1:17 in the morning and the light in the main room was still on, peaking over the tapestry separating you from me. I had texted you at 12:55 asking if you were okay out there alone because it had been about an hour or so. And I hate using terms like texting and calling in my writing, but I realize that it's a modern day way of communicating and there's nothing poetic about how pathetic I am in my moments of emotional vulnerability.

I slid into place and buried my face into a scratchy purple throw blanket. I watched your chest rise and fall. I almost had it all. But I didn't. I felt as if I had nothing. And as I listened to Nils Frahm and began drifting, I heard a sound and it sounded like my feelings and what I was listening to was "Is Love What You Don't Know" and I cried for a moment, silently of course. Then returned to watching your limp corpse rise and fall to your breathing and I drifted into something deeper than my desire to kiss you.

It's funny because when I woke up at 5:49, I wasn't tired. I had slept in a chair under twenty pounds of downy blanket and cotton stuffing since 1:27 that morning, but I didn't feel a thing. I saw you gently folding something and quietly sliding it into your back which I had broken the zipper off of. We did not speak. Just made eye contact and I came to terms with the fact that... I would never be kissing you. But I still wanted to.

(The pain was never beautiful. It hurts some days more than others. My chest implodes and my mind runs in circles so much so that the film it replays ties itself in knots and the feet of my logical thinking get twisted and dizzy and the pain is never beautiful. The pain is never beautiful. It just is.)

7.5.16

I'm looking at her. My heart pushes against the back of my ribs as it beats violently and I can't tell if it's from the fireworks, or her. She sites with her knees tucked up against her delicate chest that heaves soothingly up and down as she sighs. The lights are reflecting and bouncing off of her mixed blue eyes. She looks like a child struck with amazement and awe. Like the night sky is a black board and the explosions are colored bullets being shot upon it, bursting with vibrant light and running down the side. The fireworks make the sky appear as though it has limits, just like her eyes make the ocean appear as though it has only ever been a puddle in comparison to the infinite sea of her. Her. Her slender hands, her bony wrists and fingers grasp her kneecaps and keep them close, as if she can't let herself get away. She won't rest her chin though. She throws her head back, like when she laughs. She just watches. Eyes fixed on the sky, forever. And as the white blinding explosions begin to open fire, I realize that I'm going to die someday and none of this will have been real. Not to anyone but me. And it may have happened, but it wasn't real. None of it was real. Because in this moment, both nothing, and everything matters.

Made in the USA
Middletown, DE
26 October 2018